AT GLEASON'S GYM

AT GLEAS

ON'S GYM

TED LEWIN

A NEAL PORTER BOOK
ROARING BROOK PRESS
NEW MILFORD, CONNECTICUT

AT GLEASON'S GYM the world works out. It's down on the Brooklyn waterfront just a left hook away from the Brooklyn Bridge. It's the most famous boxing gym in the world. World champions like Muhammad Ali and Jake La Motta, "The Raging Bull," have trained there. And like Sugar Boy, at nine years old, the best little fighter around, the winner of the State Silver Gloves, and the Ringside Nationals and three-time winner of the Elite Team Junior Olympics. It builds bodies, confidence and courage.
It's everybody's gym.

Sugar Boy heads up the concrete stairs to the second floor of an old loft building. He pulls open the big steel door that says GLEASON'S GYM and . . .

The noise and smell of sweat hit you
in the face like a roundhouse right.

Kickboxers from Thailand, girl boxers, big, burly wrestlers—four rings full of action: three for boxing, one for training professional wrestlers.

RATATATATA TA T/
RATATATATATATA
THUMP THUMP
THUMP THUMP!

Heavy bags swing wildly.
Speed bags blur.

BZZZZZZZZW!

Start of a round.

Squeak of soles on canvas,
the music of the gym.

Guys jump rope and shadowbox with monsters in fun-house mirrors.

Acres of black metal lockers glint in the dim light. The air smells like a thousand worn sneakers. One super bag the size of a side of beef swings on its chain. If you train on *that*, who are you expecting to fight? Sugar Boy bobs and weaves and throws a combination at it.

BAM BAM BAM!

"Hey, Sugar Boy! How long you been comin' here?"
"Since I'm two years old."
That's when he remembers headgear being plopped on his head for the first time.

POP POP! SMACK!

A young woman with her trainer gets ready for a sparring match.

Everyone around Sugar Boy jabs and dances to his own tune. He jokes with a young kid unwrapping his hands after a workout. The red wraps hang from his wrists like kite tails as they're unwound.

BNNNN!

Then Sugar Boy watches a match from ringside. He stands just behind a young Russian girl with close-cropped hair, broad shoulders and oversized boxing shorts. Her eyes, like everyone else's, are trained on the action.

Round over! Now it's her turn. Her trainer spreads the ropes, and she steps into the ring. As she spars with her partner most of the crowd yells in Russian. Sugar Boy yells in English.

The gym is a mass of men, women, and kids dancing, bobbing, weaving and jabbing. Jump ropes—*tip tap tip tap tip tap*. Duck, jab, bob, jab, weave, jab, bob, jab, duck. Focus pads—*bam bam BAM!*

A father wraps the hands and wrists of his five-year-old daughter, and they spar for a while in another ring. She throws punches, hitting him hard in the stomach, laughing all the while. She can't reach any higher.

Sugar Boy can't stand still.
He bounces up and down and
swivels his head around.

After his father wraps his hands, he lightly
jabs and punches everything and everyone—
the old, headless rubber dummy, anyone
walking by, the heavy bag, the pad on
the ring post.

He dances the length
of the gym, then back
again, backward.

He trains six days a week. Stretches,
shadowboxing, heavy bag, focus
pads and sparring. On the seventh
day he runs.

Now it's Sugar Boy's turn in the ring. He shares it with a big middleweight pro. They spar good-naturedly. They look like David and Goliath. Someone yells to the middleweight, "Better watch out! That's Sugar Boy you're messin' with." They all laugh.

His father, a professional fighter himself, calls out, and Sugar Boy gets serious and starts shadowboxing around the ring. His father watches him intently from the corner, head tipped to one side, then stops him. "Don't drop your right hand before you jab." Sugar Boy listens, his brow furrowed and dripping with sweat. *Buzzzzzzzz!* Round over.

His father enters the ring with the focus pads.

BZZZZZ!

Round begins.

Sugar Boy's punches are sharp and clean. *Pop, pop, POP!* into the pads. He backs his father into the corner and his punches come in blurs. "Keep your right up," his father says quietly.

BZZZZZZ!

Round over. Sugar Boy, soaked with sweat, goes to the corner, dancing from foot to foot, unable to stand still even to rest. Then he jumps out of the ring and heads for the speed bag.

"Hey, Sugar Boy! You ever train anywhere else?"

"Nah, been here too long to leave."

A slight, nine-year-old girl has her hands wrapped by her trainer. It's her second lesson. She shadowboxes, "doing rotations." Hands up, jab jab, turn, jab jab, turn.

With gloves now, it's on to the focus pads. Her trainer shows
her how to move from side to side and to bob and weave.
She listens intently, eyes glued to him as she moves.
"They're easy to teach," her trainer says with a smile.

It's Saturday morning and the sun is pouring in the big glass windows. The gym is packed. A group of five-year-olds is punching the rubber dummies, and a tiny six-year-old works on the speed bag.

A tall, skinny girl works on the focus pads in one of the rings. Her punches are quick and clean. *Bam, bam, BAM!*

Suddenly, the gym is quiet. The only
sound is the soft clank of a barbell,
like a grace note.

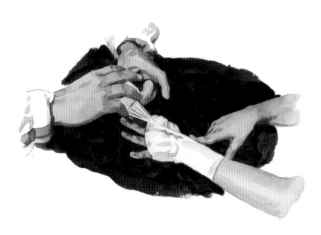

Sugar Boy comes in with his father. The beat picks up again. The state Silver Glove tournaments are coming up, and Sugar Boy is well conditioned and sharp. He will spar every other day, then every day, as the tournament gets closer. His father carefully wraps Sugar Boy's hands, twisting tendrils of adhesive tape between the fingers, then anchoring them to the wrists. Finally, a thick wad of padding is taped over the knuckles.

They talk about school. Sugar Boy loves science and social studies. His father says quietly, "A good brain in a good body." The gloves are pulled on and taped to the wrists. A boy Sugar Boy's age walks over with his trainer. The boy is to be Sugar Boy's sparring partner. They touch gloves and nod. This three-round training session will test all those hours of instruction, focus pads and shadowboxing.

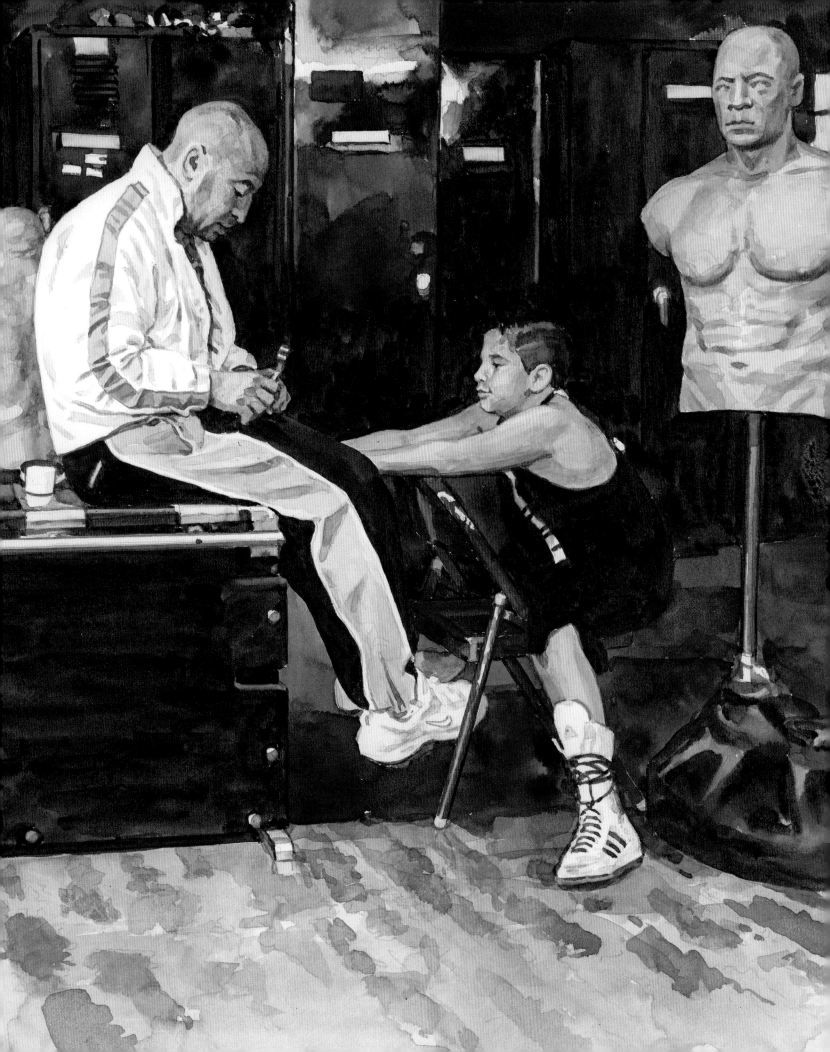

They're in the ring now. *Buzz!* Round begins. Everyone in the gym comes to watch.

Trainers yell instructions: "Breathe! Breathe! Now work! Work!" They clinch and roll along the ropes.

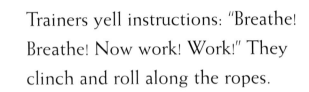

They break, and Sugar Boy drops his hands, dances sideways, chews on his mouthpiece, pushes his headgear back with both gloves, and lets rip with a terrific combination. Near the end of the third round, Sugar Boy has his opponent in the corner. They clinch, and Sugar Boy yells out through his mouthpiece to nobody in particular, "THIS IS FUN!"

BZZZZZZ!

The round is over. The crowd cheers. Sugar Boy's
dad pulls off his gloves and unwraps his hands.
Then they all go back to making the music
of the gym.

TIP TAP   TIP TAP   TIP TAP

SMACK!

SMACK!

BAM BAM

BAM!

Tomorrow is another day closer to the state championship for Sugar Boy. If he wins there, it's on to the nationals in Independence, Missouri. A win there will make him number one in the country in the 110-pound bantamweight division.

But first, more shadowboxing, more focus pads, more heavy-bag work as Sugar Boy finds his own notes to add to the music.

He's got a good brain in a good body,
and he uses both . . .
at Gleason's Gym.

Sugar Boy Younan
National Silver Gloves Champion
110 Pound Bantam Weight Division
Independence, Missouri
February 4, 2006

GLOSSARY

Break: When opponents let go of each other and back away from a clinch.

Clinch: Gripping the opponent's body, pinning his arms to his sides so he can't punch.

Combination: A series of punches.

Focus pads: Large, flat padded gloves worn by a trainer. The boxer throws punches into the pads.

Head gear: Protective helmet made of padded leather.

Hook: A short blow delivered with the elbow bent.

Mouthpiece: A rubber insert bitten down on to protect one's teeth

Round: A segment of time. In amateur boxing, three minutes.

Roundhouse: A punch delivered with a sweeping sidearm movement.

Shadowbox: To spar with an imaginary opponent.

Spar: A practice boxing match.

Speed bag: A small punching bag.

For Bruce Silverglade of Gleason's Gym; for his wonderful trainers, and for the athletes they train. Special thanks to Sugar Boy and Sherif Younan.

Copyright © 2007 by Ted Lewin

A Neal Porter Book

Published by Roaring Brook Press

Roaring Brook Press is a division of Holtzbrinck Publishing Holdings Limited Partnership

143 West Street, New Milford, Connecticut 06776

www.roaringbrookpress.com

Distributed in Canada by H. B. Fenn and Company, Ltd.

Library of Congress Cataloging-in-Publication Data

Lewin, Ted.

At Gleason's gym / by Ted Lewin. — 1st ed.

p. cm.

"A Neal Porter book."

ISBN-13: 978-1-59643-231-4   ISBN-10: 1-59643-231-4

1. Boxing—Juvenile literature. I. Title.

GV1150.L48 2007   796.83—dc22   2006032176

Roaring Brook Press books are available for special promotions and premiums. For details, contact: Director of Special Markets, Holtzbrinck Publishers.

Printed in China

Book design by Jennifer Browne

First edition August 2007

10 9 8 7 6 5 4 3 2 1